GIRLHOOD

JULIA COPUS

Girlhood

———

ff

FABER & FABER

First published in 2019
by Faber & Faber Ltd
Bloomsbury House
74–77 Great Russell Street
London WC1B 3DA

Typeset by Hamish Ironside
Printed in the UK by TJ International Ltd, Padstow, Cornwall

The right of Julia Copus to be identified as author
of this work has been asserted in accordance with Section 77
of the Copyright, Designs and Patents Act 1988

A CIP record for this book is available from the British Library

ISBN 978-0-571-35106-0

2 4 6 8 10 9 7 5 3 1

For the girlhood
and for my large and imperfect family
with love

Without imperfection, neither you nor I would exist.
— STEPHEN HAWKING

All of the days that have opened their eyes lie staring.

– ROSALIE MOORE

Acknowledgements

Thank you to the editors of the following publications, in which some of the poems in this book first appeared: *The Compass, Granta, The Idler, New Statesman, Poetry Review* and *The Spectator*.

Thanks to my husband, Andrew Stevenson; to Colette Bryce and Jane Feaver; to the girlhood that is Iphigenia and all at the irreplaceable Helyar group – Fiona Benson, Claire Crowther, Jane Draycott, Annie Freud and Jenny Lewis; also to Matthew Hollis and Lavinia Singer at Faber, and to my agent, Georgina Capel.

For their crucial support, financial and otherwise, my thanks to Steve Cook, Eileen Gunn and the whole fellowship of writers at the Royal Literary Fund.

Thank you to the Royal Society of Literature for a fellowship in 2018, and for allowing me the privilege of signing the roll book with George Eliot's pen.

'Any Ordinary Morning' was commissioned by Carol Ann Duffy for *1914: Poetry Remembers* (Faber & Faber, 2014).

The image on page 71 is from Bubica/Shutterstock.com.

Finally, thank you to all those writers whose voices travel with me, and some of whose words (remembered and occasionally half-remembered) have surfaced in this book: John Ashbery, W. H. Auden, Gaston Bachelard, Martin Buber, Nathaniel Dorsky, Susan Greenfield, Selima Hill, Gerard Manley Hopkins, Martha Nussbaum, Ovid, Sylvia Plath, Plutarch, Propertius and William Wordsworth.

Contents

GIRLHOOD

The Grievers

At length we learned what it meant to 'come to' grief.
As if grief lay in wait for us all along,
a barricade or boulder in the road.
What was it pulled us to it – led as we were
to its cold, stone smell, its granite skin?
We knew it by the way the light had shrunk
to a frayed corona; in increments, we understood
there was nothing to do but swallow it whole
and inch our way forward again. But to find we were able –
that was the miracle. It was as if the soul,
which has no definite shape, consisted simply
of a flexible cell wall: in grief, the soul
distorts and forms a seal around the loss.
What we can't absorb we carry in us,
a lumpish residue. It's truly a wonder
we manage to move at all; let alone
as freely as this, with the ease at times
of our old and lighter selves. And when I say we . . .
Look out into the street – we are everywhere:
on bikes, at bus-stops, among the crowds
of those who have not happened yet on grief.
We steady our own like an egg in the dip of a spoon,
as far as the dark of the hallway, the closing door.
Some of us are there even now, in the dusk
that gathers behind doors. We are catching our breath,
convinced we won't be joining you again,
surprising ourselves at the last because we do.

Wolfman Jack

The teenage workers at the Spitfire factory
said they'd felt the concrete crack
under their stomachs as they lay against it

with the bombs coming down, destroying a train that
    had paused
at the station. This was a full five years before my father
was born, before the track was mended, and a good many

before we moved to that place, the freight trains passing
at the end of our narrow garden, taking their cargo of steel
sections out to the shipyard. Their quiet rumble carried

right into the lounge, to where I had been settled
one late afternoon in my favourite red
dungaree playsuit in front of *Fingerbobs*. It was the episode

where Fingermouse and Gulliver gather feathers
for an adventure set in a country full of bumps.
The lull of Yoffy's chant as he told the story blended

with the hum of my mother's, speaking into the phone
in the next room to her new man-friend until
her words got mixed instead, without any warning,

with the howl of Wolfman Jack in the skincare advert
and sent me screaming to her so she straightaway drops
the plastic handset, leaving it dangling

on its coiled flex to yo-yo by the wall. All the while
it takes to calm me, the handset goes on hanging there; it is
yellowish opaque cream, the colour of Milkybars, and soon

she lifts it again to her ear and begins the story
of why I am crying, when in the middle distance
a horn sounds twice, like a panicked animal,

from one of the endless trains that will not be there
when we move to the house where my stepfather will be
no longer just an imagined voice coming

faint and innocuous, out of the wood-chip wall.

A Thing Once it has Happened

To begin somewhere other
than at the beginning, to begin
in that last summer of the '80s, with the tutor –
his wire-wool beard, his sotto voce slights
and compliments, the meekness he affects
to say them in – and with the student, who is beautiful,
but not too beautiful – 'a little
on the thin side' – each time I reach them
the tutor is quoting a line from the poet
Propertius. It is a passage from the *Elegies*
where our screwball hero pictures Cynthia
with another man and spits the words – *rumpat
ut assiduis membra libidinibus.* 'May his cock
be broken by insatiable lust', Wire-wool
translates, the sounds in his mouth awakening
the many passions he has never spoken
for other young women, thereby conferring
on this one the crucial quality of fungibility.
The 1912 translation by H. E. Butler
is more circumspect: 'Let his insatiate lusts
break all his strength.' But 'cock'
is what the tutor says. Cock is what she hears.
She turns her head to the window
in a series of tiny jump cuts, stills
joined by infinitesimal dissolves. Beyond
the evening's rainhiss nothing
but the pulse of her ears' cicadas.

*

In the Greek pantheon, the messenger Hermes,
god of trade, of weights and measures,
is patron also of boundaries. Also, the transgression
of boundaries, in which capacity his aim
is to blur their definition: he knows
where the borders are and crosses them.
Martha Nussbaum calls such blurring
violability – where an object
(a person, say) is treated as lacking
in boundary-integrity and viewed accordingly
as something it is permissible to
break up, smash, break into.

ɗ

BEFORE

The damp space of the foyer. At waist height,
a panelled dado runs as far as the open well
of the staircase, where the quiet thickens,
as is the way with wells. Ahead
walks the tutor. The me that was then
follows, watching from the dark
theatre of my skull. The me that is now
does likewise. *The darker the space, the more
luminous the screen* (the darkness saying it).
Ahead, the barley twist balusters, the room
with its lockable two-panelled door.
Ahead, the tutor's hands depend – one on
either side, like lowered pails.

ɗ

BEFORE

Out in the cobbled –

> Wait – so now they're out?

That's right. Like this . . . Out in the cobbled streets

> But what *is* 'out'?

> Out in the cold . . . Out like a light . . .

> Out of the frame, of her hands, of her depth.

Out is vast. Is limitless. It is before.
Also provisional. Anything could.
Out in the cobbled streets a northeast wind
is blowing the June rain slantways.
Night shadows moving –

> Shadows in the dark?

Yes, from the wall lamps; soot-stained terracotta overlaced
with deeper dark – so . . . moving over the bricks
of seventeenth-century façades in a terraced row
positioned by the river. (The river, however,
from this vantage point cannot be seen.)

> Is it not generally best to consider
> that events, at any time, are poised
> to take an unexpected turn?

The shining cobbles.
The gutters running with rain.

> *I want to go back, out of the bad stories.*

> And then they arrive?

They arrive now at the department building.

> A thing once it has happened
> will always have happened.

> *It's hard to separate one time from the others.*

[8]

Three storeys, three windows, three
blocked windows to the left
of the red, gloss-painted door.
                    By which means the inside gets
                    out, the outside in.
          A rainful, black, uncertain night from the start.
He hooks a key-fob from somewhere deep in his pocket.
                    We'd like to find a way –
          Is there a way?
                    – of extending this scene.
Puts a key to the keyhole.
                    The faintest stirring of strings
                    swells then yields abruptly to a single voice.
                    Affetuoso: 'The Sibyl opened her mouth
                    and the hundred mouths of her cave.'

The Great Unburned

We're the witches you forgot to burn.

One by one we are gathering now, preparing to return
to a land divided into good, clean souls and evil
doubletalk, hexes, plump, beguiling apples.
By the moon's white eye, we'll take to the air with our
loose hair streaming, the wind a blur in our faces,
we, with our prattle and inwit, our difficult questions.
Through the small hours we'll soar, through a blizzard of stars.
The longer we journey, the more your mind chafes,
scratching away at the dark. Slow at first, over fields and fences,
over the god-fearing steeples we'll climb, our broomsticks
tight in the grip of our shameless, fantastical thighs.
How a soul of your sort longs for those dark nights! To lie
where the skies grow blacker the more you look
and the crack in the tea-cup opens a lane to the land of the dead;
where devilry skulks in the shadows, drifts on the air
that pours through the gaps in our mirrorblack windows
and only a fire will keep out the chill.
Ding, dong, bell, it's lonely in hell . . .
Back to our firelit dwellings we'll usher you,
back to the place where you thought we'd been silenced,
over the forests and down through the ages,
far from the city, the towers, the golf-course.
Hell-bent, you might say, all hush-hush we'll creep with you
into the narrowest neck of the woods. We're
hovering, watchful, on hand to lure you.
Whenever you look up, there shall we be.

Whenever you look up, there shall we be,
hovering, watchful, on hand to lure you
into the narrowest neck of the woods. We're
hell-bent, you might say, all hush-hush we'll creep with you
far from the city, the towers, the golf-course,
over the forests and down through the ages.
Back to the place where you thought we'd been silenced,
back to our firelit dwellings we'll usher you.
Ding, dong, bell, it's lonely in hell
and only a fire will keep out the chill
that pours through the gaps in our mirrorblack windows,
where devilry skulks in the shadows, drifts on the air
And the crack in the tea-cup opens / A lane to the land of the dead;
where the skies grow blacker the more you look.
How a soul of your sort longs for that place, to lie
tight in the grip of our shameless, fantastical thighs.
Over the god-fearing steeples we'll climb, our broomsticks
scratching away at the dark – slow at first, over fields and fences:
the longer we journey, the more your mind chafes.
Through the small hours we'll soar, through a blizzard of stars,
we, with our prattle and inwit, our difficult questions,
loose hair streaming, the wind a blur in our faces.
By the moon's white eye we'll take to the air, with our
doubletalk, hexes, plump, beguiling apples,
to a land divided into good, clean souls and evil.
One by one we are gathering now, preparing to return.

Any Ordinary Morning

i.m. Adolf Büker (d. 19 June 1918)

The world is as it is. This morning, for instance,
the primroses are out on the lawn, in clusters
of yellow and carmine; the lilac sways; the washing
ripples on the line. And when I lift
my orange juice to sip and set it down,
the same small chips of sunlight coalesce
on the side of my glass; the old shapes settle again

in the frame of the Kriegs-Chronik, your face at its centre
in black and white, boyish but serious –
too young beneath the spike of your Pickelhaube.
Around you the terrible names persist – Arras,
Verdun – the places you served in, rivers and towns
set in the thick black script of invocations:
Cambrai, Louvement, Monchy-le-Preux, the Scarpe . . .

Adolf Büker, it was not the soldier
in you but the lover who shaped my life.
I think of him now, the morning you left for war.
Your new young wife beside you doesn't know yet
how the story goes. Your final battle
tucked in the future still, she is laying the breakfast
unaware that already my sweetheart's grandmother
is safely landed inside her – meaning I live

not in some other world but here in this one
in which your great grandson returns each evening
at the end of both our working days, and the light
bounces off my glass any ordinary morning,
as I picture it now, catching the gold hairs
on your Marie's brown arms and flashing out
from her silver Kaffeekanne while she pours
another coffee into the kitchen's quiet.

Creation Myth

On the narrow ridge where I and Thou meet,
there is the realm of 'between'.
          – MARTIN BUBER

In days where you were not, I went as the crazed
but duteous bee goes to its tasks, my words were moths
caught under glass, my thoughts fleet as a spring
shower and you were nowhere, not in all those days
when I as a long-limbed girl started from school
for the witching hour of home, willing the road
on and on and, fear-slowed, dawdled, while the barley field
in my eye's corner – the left eye – shimmied and stilled
at the wind's whim. And again you were not there
later in the many hard-shadowed bedrooms
of almost-strangers, there least of all,
though if Buber had it right an inborn Thou
was all the while stretching a white root
into the earth of me: step-daughter, scholar,
sister, lover – all the many ways the world had then
for making sense of me, my life. My story
went on telling me – at any rate I
was being told. Some story! A brief flirtation
with the voguish North, afternoons where I sailed
under a slick umbrella *calmly on*
to one chore or another until desperation had me
questioning the choices I had made: is it possible
I might have made a go of things after all
with him? Or him? Hadn't I thought so at the time?
And sworn by it? But in the unknowable meanwhile
the sunlit length of garden where we'd meet (*how*
far from then forethought of) had shrunk to a year
away already – just a year! – its warm, brick walls; then it was
weeks only, days . . . till at last I blinked and stepped

(or – yes – was drawn, for something did stir in me, inborn
or no, at the sight of you; you'll get the moment I mean
from my having told it so often: the breezy shiver
of birch leaves at your shoulder, your voice and the blue
of your jacket, the kindlier blue of your eyes), stepped,
as I've said, without thinking, onto the narrow
ridge of our beginning, and became.

Waking late

on the day of the test – no sign
    of my beloved – I glimpse

through holes in the oleaster
    the empty driveway.

House-side of the hedge, leaf
    -shadows wave, double-

tonguing the pavestones – an
    overfed pigeon

waddles across – the hawthorn
    blossom drifting.

Past the main road not
    two miles east of here,

schools, shops, surgeries, the whole
    skylapped town is assembling.

Here – oh my darling – here, everything
    remains as it was left,

the hedge a heaving
    mass of chlorophyll, each

leaf the fruit
    of a turn in the branch,

the yard intermittently
   patterned by shadows & blossom,

the fidgety shadows,
   the lightly falling blossom.

The Week of Magical Thinking

The week she fell ill, when the war broke
inside her, antibodies advancing

on blood cells as if she were harbouring
the woods and fields she no longer

had an appetite for, and the blood cells were
those fidgety squirrels that only yesterday she'd

given chase to; the week the vet phoned out of hours
and we heard our far-off selves consenting

to the dumb, aggressive drugs that had her drinking
half her body weight in water,

I glimpsed in the scuffed and sun-warmed earth
between the gatepost and the wall a pottery shard,

roughly crescent-shaped, its scalloped rim
the usual dizzying cobalt

painted onto plates of blue and white
and bowls, cups, coffee pots the wide world over

bearing the maiden and her outlawed lover,
the zigzag fence, the dripping willow branches,

the couple's swift, miraculous escape
across the triple-arched bridge, towards the future.

Without a future, I thought, *there'd be*
no need of a bridge. Each time I

passed it, propped on its damaged edge
on the kitchen counter, rinsed

of the last few sticky crumbs of earth, I meant
to throw it out. There must have been countless others

lying somewhere in the dark
soil – ordinary, worthless, broken – yet only this one

had surfaced in our driveway, lain like the torn
fragment of a letter at my foot, very close to the spot

where she had used to lie against the gate. Not long ago
it was a risk to leave the gate ajar,

so eager was she to be up and
bounding into the day. Now nothing

would coax her from the house but still
the village children stopped to search for her

forbearing gaze beneath the lowest bar, her chin
stretched on its cushion of paws, her famous nose

moving endlessly to feast on the air,
and the million beckoning odours drifting there.

Sunday Morning at Oscar's

I'd left the village to its farrago
of dog walkers, devil dodgers and kids
hurling their cries and compact bodies
skywards on the Vanderplanks'
endlessly lissom trampoline
and made for town. My catabolic nerves
had run me ragged – which is how I found myself,
goosed and fretful, pootling
among the mirrored pillars and caramel-
coloured wood panelling of Oscar's. Once again
it amazes me how easily I may be soothed
by orderly rows of hosiery! The trick
is to give yourself up to the calm of it, the white
and the black packets, each one forward facing, ranged
as in a child's bookcase – Oh Mr Wordsworth,
I say aloud, the world is not *enough* with us,
and am drawn immediately to the silken samples
that hang on the wall, head-height, like trophy tails and
soon I'm stretching one over my hand, and then
another, trying them for colour: *nearly nude,*
powder, noisette, illusion. I go on
up the steps to Cosmetics, and am happy there
for a good five minutes painting earnest stripes
on the back of my left hand in shades of coral
and pink (lately I'm in thrall
to my ersatz sense of otherness – praise be
for the narcissism of small differences!).
The silver lipstick boxes ranked
like terracotta soldiers lightly
joggle, lightly right themselves again
as I open the commodious drawer,

lift out a luminous *Rose Boudoir* and seeing
the tills deserted drop the packet
into my mackintosh pocket. Then how quickly
it begins to feel at home there! Nested,
like an egg. Two naked alabaster mannequins
recede behind me as I trace my steps
back over the blonde carpet. Near the exit
three shoulder bags the size of small dogs crouch,
straight out of one of my pellucid dreams,
on a low wood table, and I'm back in the street
with the pramfaces, the kooks and mavericks, lank,
slope-shouldered desperados, some of them turning
with me now into the passage of Magdalene Walk
where above us the vast, closed-petalled winds
of late mid-morning cluster and I push my feet
one after the other on then on a little
quicker than usual, because it looks like rain.

So Long

Don't mind the clatter: it's my infant
        father, trailing a tin-can train
from room to room through a draughty
        Dundee parsonage – kitchen
to scullery, and back again.

He totters as far as the broken wooden table-
        top, propped at the wall, then through
the gap between the wood and the open
        toolbox round which he must manoeuvre
string and train and him. – There's the roguish screw

on the table's underside, on which he will
        impale his hand as he trips but
keeps from falling. I've pictured it often:
        the steel tip sinking
through the flesh of his four-year-old palm.

He prevails, advances to the era of *Boy's Own*,
        electronics tricks and Dan Dare, *No. 1*
space hero, Pilot of the Future!
        All this was in the days before the dooms
and disappearances, falls he couldn't

break: the bloom and wither
        of a marriage too soon over-
blown, the games his daughter brought
        from the playground: French elastic,
fivestones, two-ball, *One man went to mow . . .*

and the changeable weather
    of the high streets: Thresher, Comet,
Woolworths, Phones 4U, Blockbuster – *Everything*
    must go! And did, each time
with feeling, like the putting out of candles

on an altar, edge to centre. At the final
    telling words too proved unequal
to the task of staying put: *croquet, cassette*
    and *cheerio.* So long,
                so long.
But that is still to happen. Now the sting

arrives: the high notes flare
    and catch, become the howl that rises
into the homely air
    as the blood ascends
to the site of the wound

near to where the hand is joined
    to the wrist, to the left
of the lunate bone where by and by
    a scar, very faint – a distant
but reachable star – will form and remain.

Some Questions for Later

What about you, North Baddesley?
Are the night watchmen there still, performing
their spins and quarter-spins in the hut
at the gates of the chemical factory?
They claimed they could see
right in through my bedroom window.
Look for yourself, they said, pointing.
There it was, three houses along,
the little, high-up porthole of my room.
                    That soon had you hurrying home.
I hurried in my sleep to morning-time.
Outside, a wispy day-moon hung
unnoticed, like a torn – no, melting –
rice-paper wafer, over scenes it could neither
alter nor illuminate.
                    The way you put it, midnight
                    is morning, morning afternoon.
That's how it is. None
of the clocks here
is turning. Not a one.
                    (As in – *What's the time, Mr Wolf?*
                    It's NONE o'clock!)
In the holidays my flinty shadow
stretched, loping, along your pavements,
and more than once struck laughter
from a street corner.
                    That was you? I heard it!
                    The sound flared like . . .
                    like shook foil! Flame
                    from a match.
Sound carries further in Summer. Did I mention

this happened beside the Sperrings store?
Where else? The kids
that gathered there. Smoking!
I smoked too, but I did it alone.
O dolor! O me! I walked alone
under a torn, rice-paper moon!
Wrong moon. This was after dark.
And in case you're wondering it was
my vicar-grandfather who gave me the wafers.
I was eight or nine. Next time
I asked for them he growled (no doubt
through the fug of a hangover), *Ask Mrs C.*
Mrs C. was his wife. My grandmother.
O sweetie, she said. *You must know*
they're not for playing with. What
would your grandfather say?
The shame of asking. Shame . . .
'like a white balloon / still rolls its cry /
from room to dusty room' . . .
But that was elsewhere.
I seem to be drifting away.
No. I see you. And especially
I see the house.
The house and all it housed.
The noise that came from it!
There was talk. (I think
you didn't know that.)
In the factory canteen.
What can I say? That it
was a loud house: trumpet,
French horn, violin,

piano, cello. Rage.
That bad things happened there.
That they are happening still.
That sometimes it seals itself up, will not
be got into. Other times, the opposite.
It opens and spreads, so that to move
around it requires a greater
elasticity of dreaming.
     And all the locks are broken.
     The bathroom and the loo.
     Your bedroom door.
Yes. And that. But it doesn't
stop me returning.
It might be the reason, even.
Sometimes I do it at will.
     You do it so it feels real!
If I press my ears
till all is seasound, white noise,
that's how the factory's hiss arrives,
and with it the sharp phenol smell
that streamed from the great
chimneys. Into the garden, in
through the open windows.
Escape from the smell was impossible.
     Resistance futile!
A house can get too porous. Everyone
in everyone else's business.
I drew in my horns, developed early
a liking for corners, edges, the hemmed-
in back seats of buses, library stacks.
But tonight I'm younger. I am about

to leave, late, with no
sub in my pocket for Brownies in the squat
mission church on Rownhams Road
                . . . where Brown Owl says, *Hop*
                twice around the toadstool!
Yes. I'd forgotten that.
                The usual penance. She has made a note.
And the hall is echoey with the voices
of little girls, the windows set high
like projectionists' booths. Through them, dusk
is turning the sky a brilliant shade of crimson
enriched by smoke from the melting tonnes
of resins, sealants, glues and that sticky
vinyl cling-film Stepfather produced one day
for my mother, with a conjuror's flourish.
                It clung to everything!
He thumped the box on the counter,
as if he were presenting her with the answer
to end all answers – which, in a sense,
he was. I have seen these things
many times over. I wrap them
in language and make a gift
of them. But what am I left with? I am left
with the old questions, such as what
happens in the voids, the unlit
spaces, when our backs are turned?
And do the gaps grow in the dark,
unseen, as mushrooms do? *Proliferate?*
If it's true that memory is Janus-
faced and looks to the future I would like
very much to meet its gaze but I

am elsewhere now – as in the famous case
of 'Madame I' – can no longer feel
my arms, my legs, my head and my hair.
I have to check myself constantly.

This is a true and honest account
of the facts. From such a distance
I am as worn (therefore every bit
as pointless) as that wafery moon,
and like her cannot keep
from coming back to witness
what will not be altered. Once
again somebody somewhere
is getting away with murder.

Acts of Anger

I knew a girl. Her Gaffer was out of the house for the
  morning, a Saturday.
When her friend called round to play they had the idea
of making a cake. It was the Gaffer's birthday.

The girl did not much like the Gaffer – naturally: she was
  afraid of him.
But a cake would be fun. Better, it would be insurance
against the charge that she lacked respect.

So here they are, standing at a kitchen counter, facing front:
two twelve-year old girls. On the worktop
is an opened packet

of Betty Crocker's Stir 'n Frost chocolate cake mix and
a large stoneware mixing bowl. Fluorescent light
bathes the counter and adjacent area.

> Plutarch compares the person who is quick to
> anger with a length of weakened iron. An excess
> of anger creates in the soul an evil state which
> he calls ὀργιλότης – 'irascibility' – evidenced by
> 'sudden outbursts of rage, moroseness, and
> peevishness when the temper becomes ulcerated,
> easily offended, and liable to find fault for even
> trivial offences, like a weak, thin piece of iron
> which is always getting scratched'.

The girl pours the cake mix from the cut cellophane packet.
    Out it shuffles.
How is *that* going to make a chocolate cake? the friend asks,
peering into the bowl. It's nearly as pale as you. (*Giggles.*)

> In the presence of such a soul, the ability to escape
> becomes of paramount importance. Out the front
> door. Never mind the shoes.

The girl cracks eggs on the rim of the mixing bowl,
    tips them in
while the friend stirs. Then the oil. Then the water.
The mixture starts to resemble

the glossy mud with which she made mud-cakes in days
    before the Gaffer.
This is more like it, says the friend.
The girl takes her turn

with the wooden spoon, smoothing out lumps as she goes.
The tins are greased, the oven is
warm and waiting.

II

> Many cultures see human anger as something
> outside us; a force of nature, as in *A storm is
> brewing. It was a stormy encounter.* There is some-
> thing collusive about the widespread use of such
> phrases. They seem to me a flagrant abdication of
> responsibility.

In the quiet of the girl's bedroom, the girl and her friend sit
side by side on the bed, their backs to the wall,
sharing cold baked beans from a can.

The chocolate cake has been placed, iced but undecorated,
on the white kidney-shaped dressing table.
Are you sure there's time

to get to the shops? asks the friend. Of course.
What if he comes back while we're out
and finds the cake?

He won't come in here. The girl reaches for a stack
of yellow Post-it Notes. Her blue felt-tip
writes greenish on the page –

SURPRISE! DO NOT ENTER!!! She adds a smiley face,
and puts the note aside; returns to the beans. (*A pause.*)
God, these beans are disgusting. (*Giggles.*)

> Shakespeare's *Henry VIII* is full of anger – 'choler'
> and 'flow of gall'. In only the second scene, the
> Duke of Norfolk turns to Buckingham and tells
> him, 'Anger is like / A full-hot horse; who being
> allowed his way, / Self-mettle tires him.' Odd how
> pieces of horse tack creak and wink out from many
> of our anger idioms – leather bridles and reins,
> curb chains. *He could not rein in his anger. She
> must learn to curb her temper. They bridled at the
> suggestion.* In every case, the horse is the anger; the
> owner of the horse the angry person. Again, the

analogy strikes me as evasive. It wasn't me, Your
Honour: it was my horse.

III

Walking home from the shops, the girl is clutching two small
    paper bags:
in one there is a tube of Smarties, and a pair of small jelly
    hands;
in the other, birthday candles.

As they reach the house, the door gets sucked
back into it. *Implodes.* In the gap stands
the Gaffer, his red

hair blazing, eyes too. The impression is of nothing so much
as a rearing horse. *IT'S MY BIRTHDAY
AND YOU-*

*'RE UP THERE TREATING YOURSELF TO A LITTLE
    FEAST!*
His voice is thunderous. *ON. MY. BIRTHDAY.*
The friend turns heel and runs.

The girl begins to protest. Too late: the air is already curdling
with the iron-tang of insults
and obscenities.

> The association of red with anger is ubiquitous,
> and it turns out there may be a psychological

basis. In a study conducted at North Dakota State University, participants were shown faded pictures that were a mix of red and blue – neither fully one colour nor the other. People with aggressive tendencies were more inclined to describe the pictures as red. In a sister study, subjects were asked how they might behave in a series of threatening scenarios. Red-preferring people were more likely to report that they would harm another person than those who preferred blue.

At this point, a fissure appears in the story. The girl
    remembers only
that everyone was home by teatime – the mother
and the brothers,

that nothing was said, that her eyelids were hot and puffy
    from crying,
so that she was aware of looking out at the world
through narrowed slits.

The cake was brought to the table (by her mother?) fully
    decorated,
the two hands open in applause at the centre,
just as the girl had planned,

the candles lit – *Happy Birthday, dear Gaffer* –
the small flames tugging lightly
on their stems.

MARGUERITE

One need not be a Chamber – to be Haunted –
One need not be a House –
The Brain has Corridors – surpassing
Material place –
                              – EMILY DICKINSON

In the spring of 1931, Jacques Lacan, a trainee psychoanalyst and psychiatrist, examined Marguerite Pantaine, a postal worker who had been admitted to Sainte-Anne psychiatric hospital on the outskirts of Paris after attempting to murder the actress Huguette Duflos. Lacan met with Marguerite for almost a year, and in due course used the case as the cornerstone of the doctoral dissertation that would establish his reputation.

I

LE COUTEAU

Casebook I

Female. 38. A postal worker.
Here for repeated failure to explain
a botched attempt on the life of an actress ('X').
2 pregnancies: 1 stillbirth; 1 child
(male) survives. In speech, a gap is apparent
between the words and the markedly distant
manner of their delivery. Ward staff report
that the patient is given to answering
with the same repeated fragments
of poetry: *C'est l'heure où les douleurs*
des malades s'aigrissent (and so on). Baudelaire –
a liking which itself might indicate
a hypersexual tendency. A woman of average
intellect and ability, she harbours
grandiose ambitions. Delusional, certainly.
In from the country. As her husband states,
the patient's dreams of a more
expansive life began at puberty
and prompted, upon marriage, a move to the city.
A history of depression, notably
in the wake of both her pregnancies.
Paranoid. Manic. Self-persecutory.
Taciturn, generally. Sullen in expression.
Appetite fair. Gait normal.
Oriented to person, place and time.

Knife

an interior haunting

MARGUERITE

Evening. The air was warm for April. There were bells in it and
            loose threads of
            sirens, laughter.
            There were birds but
            not many by that hour,
            and leaf-rustle.

I stood by the stage door. I watched the shadows deepen and
      stretch out
            their thin arms. My own
            hands meanwhile went
            several times to the knife,
            my gloved thumb working
            back and forth along its spine.

The dusk had voices in it too, or else the voices were me. Be
            careful, they said, and that
            she was a danger to me:
            she had everything but
            she didn't have a child.
            God took my first –

and she would have my second. She was famous, she was a
   woman who gets
                  whatever she wants.
                  But 'X' the doctor calls her!
                  A good joke. It suits her
                  too, the barely hidden
                  smut of it – *x-sex-sex*.

I stood and at length I saw how the twilight was loosening
                  the insects from
                  their crevices and how
                  they crept about underfoot.
                  The show had ended
                  and the voices spoke

again. This is *your* stage, they said. Step up. You have the knife
                  to use, so do so. In no time
                  footsteps came then
                  and the black hole of the doorframe
                  filled with her. God knows
                  the trueness of my aim.

Consulting Room

LACAN

So here we are. It is hardly the glittering city
you journeyed to in girlhood dreams, I'd venture,
tucked in your truckle bed on your father's farm.
This room, the tall white walls and the windowless

corridors beyond them. – The ward after dark!
Each dawn returns you to a sea of beds.
You open your eyes; the day rears up to meet you.
Your thoughts swim; the same unanswerable questions –

How to set foot on a day as steep as that?
Where to position your feet? Can it be done?
Alone, the task is impossible. Beyond you.
A shame. In many ways, you are still a young woman

with your questioning eyes, your fondness for Baudelaire –
Viens, mon beau chat, sur mon coeur amoureux . . .
Well, things will go easier now; we share a goal.
In step beside your own is a second shadow

ranged against the angle of the day.
Presently, it is the path to health
with which we must concern ourselves,
the long, precipitous hill and the climbing of it.

Consulting Room

MARGUERITE

I imagined him older. He stands one side of the desk
and now and then leans across it, resting his weight
on the heels of his hands. At times he drops his voice

and talks as you might to a small, slow-witted child.
His shirtsleeves are rolled to the elbows. Muscled forearms:
a tennis player's arms. Scrubbed fingernails.

Remember your girlhood? he says. The farm? The fields?
This is a trick, and I know it. He won't catch me that way.
But I *do* remember: the cold and the nights that bloomed

too suddenly, so it seemed, and sent us
rustling back to the lighted house; the wheatfields
that darkened around us, stretching to who knows where.

In the distance, he conjures my name. *Marguerite.*
I will not fall for it. I close my ears, I sing
to myself in silence, *dee, didi-dee*

(this is a trick of my own) and I settle my eyes
on the picture window that hangs just left of his head.
Here, they keep even the buttercup-lit grass

confined, like shrunken meadows that crouch
beneath the buildings, dwarfed by a towering forest
of brick walls – I have glimpsed one from where I sit,

this side of the desk, half-hidden between the vertical
slats of the blinds: a square with benches round.
No trees (they wouldn't trust us) but a brazen sun

comes streaming into it, the way his voice
streams and pools about me while the shadows reach,
thicker than prison bars, over the desk, my knees . . .

A girl could lie down in a voice like that.
Marguerite – so plain I cannot meet his eyes.
Des yeux obscurs, profonds et vastes.

And I am very tired. *Dee-dee*, I go (in my head).
Didi-dee. Didier . . . *Beaux yeux de mon enfant.*
My child. Not once does he mention my boy.

Boy

MARGUERITE

Whose birth was a light coming in, or it was rain-
water sipped into roots, a gradual suffusing
through acres of parched fields.

Whose timing was all wrong, a shadow thrown
from a monstrous wing (arriving, as he must,
in the wake of his poor dead sister).

Whose presence back then in my life was faith itself:
I saw a storm and a storm seemed tranquil;
I saw a mountain and a mountain was scalable.

Whose days now are the quiet into which bad news is spoken.
Whose boyhood is a municipal park in flower
in full, unstoppable sunshine, and I am the warden.

Whose soul is a sealed pond, peopled by skaters,
hung over fathoms of unmoving waters;
a sheet of ice with every fracture point intact.

A Lesson in Forbearance

INPATIENTS

Picture, he proposes, a puddle in sunlight
drawn up into the air by degrees, or picture
a fish lifted out of the sea, a knot of wasps
pulled from the trees to a sticky pot of jam.
We note, he says, how the catalyst itself
in every case has merely to make itself present.
Always there is concession – the fish that swims
to the baited line and bites, the puddle that yields
under the morning sun, becoming steam.

And so it is with him: so he presents himself
in front of her now and has begun to wait.

Cave

MARGUERITE

What does he want me to say? And where are the words
to conjure the cave I fashioned from my arms,
the downy warmth inside, the little head
I cupped in the palm of one hand; or the pull of the milk
that streamed through both of us, the suckling sounds
that blossomed into that cave, and the punishing wind
and wild beasts that circled somewhere beyond?

Doctor, indeed! His pleas are all to the good
but my words are buried deep and if they rose
each one would fail, the moment it emerged
from the dark of the throat: each one crackle and blister,
the way a precious child will also suffer
exposed too long to the company of strangers.

II

LE TÉLÉPHONE

The Analyst Admires his Figurines

for Annie Freud

INPATIENTS

Now, in the yellow light of the standard lamp
their small diagonal shadows stretch
from each round heel or plinth across the table
in perfect parallel – all at the same
odd angle. A decade has passed since I began
to seek them out. Each time it seemed a miracle
that they should fetch up here – from Alexandria!
Fifth century BC! Twelve pale figures,
pinkish, cool to the touch, and each one weighing
no more than this half tumbler of Balmenach.
Over time my thumb has come to know
the little bumps of their breasts and elbows, the ripple
of the rooster's comb and wattle.
The smoke that drifts from my cigar
is a rolling mist blown in from the Nile Delta
one hot afternoon. Here, a draped female
stands with her right arm held daintily
under her bosom. She might be in conversation –
the way her head is inclined – in a fig tree's cool shade,
the length of her thigh, her beautiful right foot
pointed like a fillip towards the speaker
where an overripe fruit has fallen perhaps. The smaller
male figure, seated here, has just returned
from a speech in the Mouseion; a muddle of spice
and fish smells clings to the folds
of his peplos. Or does not. All is story,
all conjecture. Do the sitters matter?
That each of them once moved in the streets of the city
among glass blowers, weavers, papyrus makers,

with their numberless gods, their ever-changing weather?
Or all except the rooster, who asserts
his puffed-out, rooster chest; the sculptor has cast him
in the prime of life, his fine coxcomb
will forever be upstanding. There isn't a price
could part me from him now – nor from the others
in their floor-length chitons of linen and silk.
Seeing them makes of the heart a fire-balloon
set afloat in the blackest nights, their fixed expressions
revealing no psychoses; every thought,
each love, regret, ambition smoothed
and defined in stone, their difficult histories.

Recollection at the Sorting Office

a haunting

MARGUERITE

When the casual staff were queuing for their wages,
squabbling over hours worked and hours

docked for lateness, I found I had nothing to do
but study those self-same wooden shelf-stacks

into whose boxy partitions I had been dealing
letters like playing cards all the long morning – a thick

and glossy forest green with the old paint peeping through,
yellow as yolk at the inside corners

of each of the twenty *arrondissements* –
Bourse, Gobelins, Hôtel-de-Ville . . .

and there by the top right edge where the smokers would
leave their cooling coffee cups on hurrying in

from the morning break was the faded label of Melun,
district of the homestead I can never forget –

the sickening heat of that other drawn-out morning:
how the telephone sang out, once and again

in a far-off room, my husband's muffled voice –
Oui? Madame Dubois! – and the bell-like pain

that divided me at last, at last, in two
when into the space in which we held our breaths

for my baby girl's full-throated cry there bloomed
instead the midwife's meagre *Vraiment désolée.*

An Appeal to the Patient

LACAN

Since you remain reluctant, let us imagine
that one's selfhood is a work of art – a maquette
in clay, as may be, and each life event
enacted by the sculptor. In he creeps
to the damp-room on his crepe-soled shoes
again and again. In time the work proceeds
via a series of flukes and inspirations:
the sculptor warms to his task; the clay responds
with little sucking sounds until it is wrapped
and laid for next time on its wooden shelf.
Nothing is done in that place that is not reparable.
Beyond the clayey dark your helpmeet is waiting.
And though his feet in the stiff grass ache with cold
he keeps, while he can, his faith; his night lamp lifted.

Dayroom I

INPATIENTS

She sits by herself in the dayroom, tracing the wallflowers
on her towelling peignoir, petals . . . stem,
and runs through all the things she will not tell him:
the marriage bed they stripped and dressed for the birth,
the mounting pain, the tarry scent of Lysol . . .

Because he has asked her please not to spare any details
and nothing, she knows, would gladden him more than to
    picture
the way her hair stuck damply to her temples
and hung in ribbony strands, her blood-streaked thighs
like two sleek seals exhausted from the journey;

or to hear how the telephone rang at just the wrong moment
and the way her husband hurried at once to answer
and how all this accounts for the death of the baby;
because it would help him, because it would please him no
    end
to gather the bits from her like fine bone china

so damaged he alone could piece them together
and to set it all down in his fluent, looping hand,
she shuts the lot inside her, where it gleams
as treasure will do, lowered into the ground,
deep, then deeper down, for no one to find.

Telephone

a haunting

MARGUERITE

Down in the hall where mother's cast-off
drop-leaf table stood, down
in the gone dark hall, above a nest
of gumboots and shoes, the telephone

held sway, for years – *years*. It had,
if I remember, a sharpish smell
like tarnish when you lifted it
and your heart went off like a kettle-drum, thun-

dering away because what might spill from it you
could never tell – and no one was there
besides the phone and you. You knew
it was a conduit for bad,

a certain *type* of evil, entirely
female. The heat of that August morning
proved it finally: my husband,
prompt as a bellboy, trotting down

to answer it; my pain; his far-off,
echoey voice . . . But that is a story
that's already been told. After that time we were
none of us fooled, not once, by its consummate

singsong pleading. Who is to say
what might be coiled inside it? Hell
would erupt, if you let it – hatch – as it did . . .
Oh, a force for ill is the telephone.

For all I know it is there – still,
gathering the voices inside it, up
to no good, for sure. When was it ever!
It will not rest: even now it is plotting,

poised on its haunches. Black Bakelite fear.
If your path takes you near it, no matter how long
and plaintively it calls, keep walking.
As fast as you like. It is not to be lifted.

Consulting Room

MARGUERITE

Talk me through that morning, he says again;
the trauma that attended the birth of your daughter.

Out there, through the glass, a lilac bush.

What changed in you? Who spoke and who said what
during those moments meant for her first cry?

Rain on the dead-beat leaves.

I ask myself, Marguerite, why it is you are stalling.
Perhaps you hope to prolong our chats together?

Hair-breadth javelins of rain, aslant on the window.

Let's start somewhere else, then. Tell me what you meant
at the very moment you placed the knife in your pocket.

Beyond, the unbending grass. Not long ago
buttercups danced there . . .
        – I couldn't imagine
        could never *begin* to imagine
        how hard he must work
        late on into the night.
        And how he is saddened.
        His work is not the kind
        that can simply be left
        like shoes at the door.

He is assembling a theory
and I am the proof of it.
I am not a good subject.
My thoughts are not
the right thoughts;
in this he is saddened.
My heart is a pickling stone;
in this he is saddened.

But determined. But saddened. Because I will not speak.

III

LA VACHE

What a dry shuffling heralds

(MARGUERITE)

is not always what you'd imagined. That first time,
dozing here in my hospital bed, it was plain
I was back in the sorting office with the girls,
the cool letters sliding again in our competent hands.

Not at all; it was only the nurses in their stiff skirts
bringing the unspeakable meal trays – every tray
adorned with a plate adorned with a greyish slop
and a limp round of vegetables next to the beaker of milk.

Sheesh, sheesh, went the letters . . . I have never forgotten
the night my husband ferried me from work
straight to dinner and drinks at La Coupole!
It was an anniversary – our first,

perhaps – the plump and gleaming aubergines
stuffed to the brink, the dizzying aromas,
cloves and cinnamon and jasmine rice.
My stomach in those days was flat as a boy's

in spite of the rare *bonne bouches* I fed it
in the candlelight those evenings. We were living
sight unseen, footloose and routeless, we were
a *folie à deux* (the nurses wouldn't get that),

our balloon hearts lifting inside us – *coeurs légers,
semblables aux ballons*. 'True travellers
are those who depart for departing's sake', I tell them –
and send the lot away. It is not what I asked for.

Dayroom II

Bit by bit discord has weakened her.
The onset of autumn wanders through the grounds
looking for things to dislodge – leaves, certainties.

Sweetbriar crowds the window. Inside, its shadow
lies twitching on the wood-tiles. All she longs for
is calm: to calm them both. She runs through it now in
    her mind –

a simple nod would do it, a concordance.
She gives the nod. So many complexities, so many
contradictions fly to their new positions

like the mice in the farmhouse
that vanished through her childhood at the sound of feet
away to their hidey holes, fleet and nimble,

to bide their time, their tiny hearts pulsing.

Casebook II

A turning point is reached. Progress begins.
This female's persecutory delusions,
coupled with alarming delusions of grandeur,
are rooted, without question,
in the birth of her first child, a stillborn daughter.
Previously taciturn, now, with little prompting,
patient recounts the trauma of that day
with peculiar clarity – the change in attitude
as abrupt as it is pronounced. A week ago
nurses' notes describe the patient 'lying
dully in bed with full and rapid pulse', also
'difficult and resistive with her diet'.
Today, at length, she is compliant:

ME: We could say the onset of anxiety coincides
      with the time of your second pregnancy.

PATIENT: I suppose we could.

ME: It was then you fashioned the notion
      that certain people – specifically, certain
      women – were intent on separating you
      from your son, or on doing him harm.

PATIENT: I did.

ME: You became convinced that 'X' –
      the actress, 'X' – was one such woman.

PATIENT: (quietly) Yes.

The vanity of her megalomaniacal illusions
is, I believe, becoming clear to her –
as well as the wild misreckoning of her fears.

Cow

There are those who have built stables
in order to trap me as a milk cow.
— MARGUERITE PANTAINE

MARGUERITE

They worked in secret, almost out of earshot:
the chafe and scrape of a saw, the tap
tap tap of a hammer and another
corner of shadows was formed; a stall, a gate . . .

Now they are done – as one
and to a man they all downed tools
and the long hush fell
then, like a cold snap.

gutta cavat lapidem

Dripping water hollows out stone.
– OVID

INPATIENTS

Stone will soften. He'd known this as clearly
as the water drop knows it – even a stone
from the wilds of the country, basalt and hefted
out of some rain-darkened backwater valley.

The weight of his pleading fell on her over
and over, the sense of her loss – each granular
slippage – responding at last, as it must,
in direct proportion to the deepening hollow.

Benediction

MARGUERITE

Where am I now? Out here am I? Out. And rocking
in my perfectly—yes I am—calm.
You are now. Calm you, Marguerite. And things are—
all of them—very far off. My boy, even.
Didier. His name like a song. Song I sing. *Dee
didi-dee.* For whom all this—And my girl too who never.
Darling girl, she, who turned up already, ah no, so so so
already gone. Long gone dead. I spilled. I said. I—
Oh Jesus, god but I was quiet keeping, sweetheart,
unto myself entirely unto you, my daughter;
while I could, I was. Inviolable. *Tell me. Say,*
the good doctor commanded. *All you know.* And
No, I won't, you can't is what I said. Said
for the longest time, and no one here denies it.
I meant to see my one and live boy safe, that was all.
I told the doctor so. Exactly. *Show me a mother*—all that
bla bla. And *Who wouldn't kill for their child?* So *Well
then, well.* These things I told. Enough of it.
But he so needly. On and on, his brimful voice,
his sly and careful ways and the brawn of his
brown arms—that indeed was the undoing, then
was the wretch of me. Wretch that I am—it is he
that thinks it—he, Doctor. His shiny-shoed going—
tap tap—feet beginning always to go even
as the nurses lead me back away. *C'est l'heure*
what is it now—*C'est l'heure*—how does it—*l'heure
où les douleurs*—But deaf his ears. Deaf
and always so, who is set to thinking
he has solved the puzzle of me. Good! And let him.

What there is of me—what left—he took and takes
but goes too with it. Off now. Off, away. And for the calm
that is here and for the elsewhere of it
ever on me now, the sure release I must and do
most justly thank him, lord. Amen, amen.

How to Eat an Ortolan

INPATIENTS

Here he is in a candled corner: a man in his off-hours.
A tablecloth (red gingham), a smoking cocotte,

an aroma – of figs, of Armagnac – so rich
that already he feels overfed. He bends to the dish,

hears the juices sizzle and subside,
then picks the bird up whole by its crisp-skinned skull,

burning his fingers, and is stirred for a moment
by its frailty (it is light as a box of matches);

places it into his mouth, but does not chew.
What we hear is the hiss of air: four seconds, five.

Now he bites – through skin, the nutty meat
of breast and wing, the snap of powdery bones.

Under the rib cage, a pea-sized heart, a lung
release their fabled liquor on his tongue.

Stories

after Marie Howe

Think of a night in midsummer, a night with water
falling to a pond from the raised mouth

of a freckled stone seal, & children up late
calling to each other two or three gardens away, & under

those a softer murmur. So lies the past,
no further. You do not need to get up

& stand on tiptoe at the hedge to know
that what you hear are the people you love. You suppose

the stories I've told are over. Think of the garden.
You sat there so long the dew had settled

on the grass, on the yellow pistils of the irises, the children's
    hair.
Their laughter was made of the same

air that moved as a breeze across you, & the dew likewise
was bits of sky, nestling where it could, & all of it

(although you could not touch it)
was part of you, was what the summer night contained.

Notes

In 'A thing once it has happened', 'I want to go back, out of the bad stories' is a quotation from John Ashbery's 'Lateral Sclerosis'. Martha Nussbaum's use of the term 'violability' in the context described in this poem comes from a subsection of her 1995 essay 'Objectification' entitled 'Seven Ways to Treat a Person as a Thing'.

The epigraph to 'The Great Unburned' is a banner slogan from the Women's March on Washington following Donald Trump's presidential inauguration. The line 'And the crack in the tea-cup opens / A lane to the land of the dead' is from W. H. Auden's 'As I Walked Out One Evening'.

In 'Some questions for later', the quoted poem-fragment 'like a white balloon . . .' is from Selima Hill's 'Shame'. A description of the fascinating case of 'Madame I' can be found in Susan Greenfield's *You & Me: The Neuroscience of Identity* (Notting Hill Editions, 2017).

In 'Acts of Anger', the citation that begins 'sudden outbursts of rage . . .' is from Plutarch's *De cohibenda ira, Plutarchi Moralia*, section 3, translated by W. C. Helmbold.

'Marguerite': The French passages in this sequence are from Baudelaire's *Les Fleurs du mal*. They may be translated as follows:

'Consulting Room (Lacan)': '*Viens, mon beau chat, sur mon coeur amoureux*' – 'Come, my beautiful cat, lie down on my infatuated heart'.

'Consulting Room (Marguerite)': '*Des yeux obscurs, profonds et vastes*' – 'dark eyes, deep and vast'; '*Beaux yeux de mon enfant*' – 'the beautiful eyes of my child'.

'Casebook I': '*C'est l'heure où les douleurs des malades s'aigrissent*' – 'This is the hour when the sorrows of the sick grow bitter'.

The title 'gutta cavat lapidem' is from Ovid, *Epistulae ex Ponto* IV, 10, 5.